TITLE: PRINT YOUR OWN MONEY

TABLE OF CONTENT

INTRODUCTION

Money is attracted by the value offered. The higher the value, the more the money. Money does not respond to wishes, tears nor prayers or fasting. Money is in the hands of people and to get it you must have a service or a product to offer to them. Money is a means of exchange and differs based on the country you are in. Jumping from one place to another is not the solution, offering value where you are is all you need. You see money moving to the hands of people, it can move into your hands when you offer value and package it in products or services. That's how to print your own money.

Ecclesiastes 10:19
money answereth all things.

CHAPTER ONE: ISAAC

There was a famine in the time of Isaac and like most people, he thought of going to another place to find a solution. God had to appear to him and gave him a new mindset of staying where he was and offering value there. Isaac obeyed, stayed in the land that looked so dry and sowed seeds there. The harvest he got was so much that he became very rich until non-believers envied him. Isaac printed his own money.

Genesis 1:1-6, 12-17

There was a famine in the land, besides the first famine that was in the days of Abraham. **And Isaac went to Abimelech, king of the Philistines, in Gerar.**
Then the Lord appeared to him and said: "Do not go down to Egypt; live in the land of which I shall tell you. Dwell in this land, and I will be with you and bless you; for to you and your descendants I give all these lands, and I will perform the oath which I swore to Abraham your father. And I will make your

descendants multiply as the stars of heaven; I will give to your descendants all these lands; and in your seed all the nations of the earth shall be blessed; because Abraham obeyed My voice and kept My charge, My commandments, My statutes, and My laws."

So Isaac dwelt in Gerar. Then Isaac sowed in that land, and reaped in the same year a hundredfold; and the Lord blessed him. The man began to prosper, and continued prospering until he became very prosperous; for he had possessions of flocks and possessions of herds and a great number of servants. So the Philistines envied him. Now the Philistines had stopped up all the wells which his father's servants had dug in the days of Abraham his father, and they had filled them with earth. And Abimelech said to Isaac, "Go away from us, for you are much mightier than we."

Then Isaac departed from there and pitched his tent in the Valley of Gerar, and dwelt there.

Isaac wanted to go to Egypt because he had heard his father had gone there when there was famine in his time. What Isaac forgot was that that was his father's way of printing his money, he had to discover his. Comparison denies people the opportunity to be original and create new products and services. Everybody is trying to be like the other and living this way attracts a lot of jealousy. Those who are the original creators print their own money without struggling while those who try to copy them find it hard to do so and they are full of envy, jealousy and evil thinking.

James 3:13-18
Who is wise and understanding among you? Let him show by good conduct that his works are done in the meekness of wisdom. But if you have bitter envy and self-seeking in your hearts, do not boast and lie against the truth.This wisdom does not descend from above, but is earthly, sensual, demonic. For where

envy and self-seeking exist, confusion and every evil thing are there. But the wisdom that is from above is first pure, then peaceable, gentle, willing to yield, full of mercy and good fruits, without partiality and without hypocrisy. Now the fruit of righteousness is sown in peace by those who make peace.

A fish doesn't have to be a bird for it shines in the water. Putting a fish on the land will kill it. This is what most people are doing, they are dying in areas they went to in the name of competition. Stay in your area and you will find the grace is sufficient there.

2nd corinthians 10:12
For we dare not number ourselves, or compare ourselves, with some who commend themselves. For in measuring themselves by themselves, and **comparing themselves among themselves, they are not wise.**

Ephesians 4:7

But to each one of us grace was given according to the measure of Christ's gift.

In the race every runner runs on their lane. Everybody has a lane marked for their destiny. Instead of running the race, many try to jump into other people's lanes while others stop running their race and do everything to stop those running.

Hebrews 12:1-2
Therefore we also, since we are surrounded by so great a cloud of witnesses, let us lay aside every weight, and the sin which so easily ensnares us, and **let us run with endurance the race that is set before us,** looking unto Jesus, the author and finisher of our faith, who for the joy that was set before Him endured the cross, despising the shame, and has sat down at the right hand of the throne of God.

1st Corinthians 9:24-27

Do you not know that those who run in a race all run, but one receives the prize? Run in such a way that you may obtain it. And everyone who competes for the prize is temperate in all things. Now they do it to obtain a perishable crown, but we for an imperishable crown. Therefore I run thus: not with uncertainty. Thus I fight: not as one who beats the air.But I discipline my body and bring it into subjection, lest, when I have preached to others, I myself should become disqualified.

CHAPTER TWO: EXCELLENCE

The fact that there is a product and service to be offered is not a guarantee that you will print your own money. You have to package them with excellence.

Proverbs 22:29
Do you see a man who excels in his work? He will stand before kings; He will not stand before unknown men.

Daniel served different kings in his time and all kings found him valuable. He did everything with excellence.

Daniel 5:12
Forasmuch as **an excellent spirit**, and knowledge, and understanding, interpretation of dreams, and shewing of hard sentences, and dissolving of doubts, were found in the same Daniel, whom the king named Belteshazzar: now let Daniel be called, and he will shew the interpretation.

Daniel 6:3

Then this Daniel was preferred above the presidents and princes, because an excellent spirit was in him; and the king thought to set him over the whole realm.

The spirit of God is a spirit of excellence. He was there during creation and he created the world with excellence.

Isaiah 12:5
Sing to the Lord,
For He has done excellent things;
This is known in all the earth.

All believers have the spirit of excellence so there is no excuse why your products and services cannot stand out as distinguished.

Psalms 16:3
As for the saints who are on the earth,
"They are the excellent ones, in whom is all my delight."

Solomon built the temple and his palace with the spirit of God granting him wisdom. His works were so excellent that all kings came to see the excellence of his kingdom.

1st kings 10:4-5
And when the queen of Sheba had seen all the wisdom of Solomon, the house that he had built, the food on his table, the seating of his servants, the service of his waiters and their apparel, his cupbearers, and his entryway by which he went up to the house of the Lord, there was no more spirit in her.

When you operate with the spirit of excellence, you will find that kings are attracted by the value you offer. King's reward is not the same as common people, therefore, aim to serve kings even if you may start small.

Isaiah 60:3
The Gentiles shall come to your light,
And kings to the brightness of your rising.

Rich people have a starting point, don't despise yours but also don't be comfortable with the little results. The realm where you serve kings should be the end goal.

Psalms 113:7-8
He raises the poor from the dust
and lifts the needy from the ash heap;
he seats them with princes,
with the princes of his people

CHAPTER THREE: DESPISE

In the world where everybody is following the ordinary path, the moment you choose to go on the road less travelled, the society makes you feel awkward. Goliath was used to fighting army men until David showed up looking completely opposite of what he was used to. He despised him and used words to undermine him but david knew what he had to offer. He presented it to Goliath and won the battle in a new way, using a sling and a stone.

1st samuel 17:41-51

Meanwhile, the Philistine, with his shield bearer in front of him, kept coming closer to David. He looked David over and saw that he was little more than a boy, glowing with health and handsome, and _he despised him_. He said to David, "Am I a dog, that you come at me with sticks?" And the Philistine cursed David by his gods. "Come here," he said, "and I'll give your flesh to the birds and the wild animals!"

David said to the Philistine, "You come against me with sword and spear and javelin, but I come against you in the name of the Lord Almighty, the God of the armies of Israel, whom you have defied. This day the Lord will deliver you into my hands, and I'll strike you down and cut off your head. This very day I will give the carcasses of the Philistine army to the birds and the wild animals, and the whole world will know that there is a God in Israel. All those gathered here will know that it is not by sword or spear that the Lord saves; for the battle is the Lord's, and he will give all of you into our hands."

As the Philistine moved closer to attack him, David ran quickly toward the battle line to meet him. Reaching into his bag and taking out a stone, he slung it and struck the Philistine on the forehead. The stone sank into his forehead, and he fell facedown on the ground.

So David triumphed over the Philistine with a sling and a stone; without a sword in his hand he struck down the Philistine and killed him.

 David ran and stood over him. He took hold of the Philistine's sword and drew it from the sheath. After he killed him, he cut off his head with the sword.

That's the power of believing in yourself when everybody else despises what you have. You have to be fully persuaded before you persuade others.

Romans 4:21
Being fully persuaded that God had power to do what he had promised.

Most people despise what they have. A woman was in debt and her husband had died in poverty while they had the product in their house but they didn't value it. The day she valued the oil product she had, she was able to print her own money. She paid all her debtors and got more to live on. That's how she experienced financial freedom.

2nd kings 4:1-7
The wife of a man from the company of the prophets cried out to Elisha, "Your servant my husband is dead, and you know that he revered the Lord. But now his creditor is coming to take my two boys as his slaves."
Elisha replied to her, "How can I help you? **Tell me, what do you have in your house?"**
"Your servant has nothing there at all," she said, **"*except a small jar of olive oil.*"**
Elisha said, "Go around and ask all your neighbours for empty jars. Don't ask for just a few. Then go inside and shut the door behind you and your sons. Pour oil into all the jars, and as each is filled, put it to one side."
She left him and shut the door behind her and her sons. They brought the jars to her and she kept

pouring. When all the jars were full, she said to her son, "Bring me another one."
But he replied, "There is not a jar left." Then the oil stopped flowing.
She went and told the man of God, and he said, "Go, sell the oil and pay your debts. You and your sons can live on what is left."

When the master gave talents to his servants. Two valued what they had, they traded it and got double of what they had. They found a way to print their money. One servant however, decided to hide his talent for he saw no value in it or in the one who gave it to him. He despised what he had and he ended up losing all he had.

Luke 19:11-26
Now as they heard these things, He spoke another parable, because He was near Jerusalem and because they thought the kingdom of God would appear immediately. Therefore He said: "A certain nobleman

went into a far country to receive for himself a kingdom and to return. So he called ten of his servants, delivered to them ten minas, and said to them, *__Do business till I come.__* But his citizens hated him, and sent a delegation after him, saying, 'We will not have this man to reign over us.'

"And so it was that when he returned, having received the kingdom, he then commanded these servants, to whom he had given the money, to be called to him, so that he might know how much every man had gained by trading. **Then came the first, saying, 'Master, your mina has earned ten minas.' And he said to him, 'Well done, good servant; because you were faithful in a very little, have authority over ten cities.' And the second came, saying, 'Master, your mina has earned five minas.' Likewise he said to him, 'You also be over five cities.'**

"Then another came, saying, 'Master, here is your mina, which I have kept put away in a handkerchief. For I feared you, because you are an austere man. You collect what you did not deposit, and reap what

you did not sow.' And he said to him, 'Out of your own mouth I will judge you, you wicked servant. You knew that I was an austere man, collecting what I did not deposit and reaping what I did not sow. Why then did you not put my money in the bank, that at my coming I might have collected it with interest?'

"And he said to those who stood by, 'Take the mina from him, and give it to him who has ten minas.'

(But they said to him, 'Master, he has ten minas.')

'For I say to you, that to everyone who has will be given; and from him who does not have, even what he has will be taken away from him.

CONCLUSION

Some people may say,"I have no product or service to offer for me to be able to print my own money."
No person is empty, there is something you have only that you have not discovered yet. God created the whole world with words which are a product of thoughts/ideas. Maybe you have the ideas and someone has the money, speak them out.

Genesis 1:1-5
 In the beginning God created the heavens and the earth. Now the earth was formless and empty, darkness was over the surface of the deep, and the Spirit of God was hovering over the waters.
 And God said, "Let there be light," and there was light. God saw that the light was good, and he separated the light from the darkness. God called the light "day," and the darkness he called "night." And there was evening, and there was morning—the first day.

Write your ideas down for that's a vision and approach people that you know will support your vision. Your provision is in the vision you have.

Habakuk 2:2-3
Then the Lord answered me and said:
"Write the vision
And make it plain on tablets,
That he may run who reads it.
For the vision is yet for an appointed time;
But at the end it will speak, and it will not lie.
Though it tarries, wait for it;
Because it will surely come,
It will not tarry.

Other people have connections of people who are willing to help. Put pride aside and honour those people. Pride is Satan's weapon to keep you in poverty. There are helpers God has put on your way, honour them by appreciating them.

1st peter 2:17
Honor all people, love the brotherhood, fear God,
honor the king.

God helps people by using other people. The earth
has been given to men by God therefore know how to
relate with those people in honour.

Psalms 115:16
The highest heavens belong to the Lord,
    but the earth he has given to mankind.

Remember, money is with people. The Lord will give
you favour with people but it's your responsibility to
honour them for you to receive the help you need in
your life.

Exodus 3:21

And I will give this people favour in the sight of the Egyptians; and it shall be, when you go, that you shall not go empty-handed.

Nobody rises without the help of people. Paul didn't become great just like that, he had barnabas who helped him.

Acts 9:26-29
When he came to Jerusalem, he tried to join the disciples, but they were all afraid of him, not believing that he really was a disciple. But Barnabas took him and brought him to the apostles. He told them how Saul on his journey had seen the Lord and that the Lord had spoken to him, and how in Damascus he had preached fearlessly in the name of Jesus. So Saul stayed with them and moved about freely in Jerusalem, speaking boldly in the name of the Lord.

Jesus had disciples in his ministry to help him. He accepted the help of the women who supported him with his disciples. He was not proud to think just because he was God's son he didn't need people.

Luke 8:1-3
After this, Jesus travelled from one city and village to another. He spread the Good News about God's kingdom. The twelve apostles were with him. Also, some women were with him. They had been cured from evil spirits and various illnesses. **These women were Mary, also called Magdalene, from whom seven demons had gone out; Joanna, whose husband Chusa was Herod's administrator; Susanna; and many other women. They provided financial support for Jesus and his disciples.**

The bible says you accept people for some have received angels without knowing.

But be careful for satan also uses people to destroy your life. Be discerning who are helpers and destroyers on your path to printing your own money.

Luke 22:3
Then Satan entered Judas, called Iscariot, one of the Twelve.

Hebrews 13:2
Be sure to welcome strangers into your home. By doing this, some people have welcomed angels as guests, without even knowing it.

JOHN 13:17
NOW THAT YOU KNOW THESE THINGS, YOU WILL BE BLESSED IF YOU DO THEM.

More Grace on you as you print your own money by discovering what of value you can offer to the world.

If you need help to study God's word, email me at pstmaryjoy@gmail.com and I will guide you through.

To get my other books in amazon, click this link
https://www.amazon.com/author/marynyandia

www.ingramcontent.com/pod-product-compliance
Lightning Source LLC
Chambersburg PA
CBHW070914220526
45466CB00005B/2216